THE
Archive Photographs
SERIES
CANVEY ISLAND

The Heritage Centre (St Katherine's Church).

THE
Archive Photographs
SERIES

CANVEY ISLAND

Compiled by
Geoff Barsby

CHALFORD

First published 1997
Copyright © Geoff Barsby, 1997

The Chalford Publishing Company
St Mary's Mill, Chalford,
Stroud, Gloucestershire, GL6 8NX

ISBN 0 7524 1108 X

Typesetting and origination by
The Chalford Publishing Company
Printed in Great Britain by
Bailey Print, Dursley, Gloucestershire

The ferry crossing as the tide starts to come in and the last horse and cart makes its way across.
Passengers await the ferry on the left, 1921.

Contents

Acknowledgements

This book is dedicated to the memory of Aubrey Stevens, a past chairman of the Canvey Historical Society, and to my wife Pat, for all her help in the production of this book.

I also wish to acknowledge the Stevens family, Arthur and Elsie Lesadd, Beryl and Harry Bear, Darrell McClure and Leanne McClure.

When appropriate I have added some longer historical background pieces to some of the picture captions in the book which local readers may recognise as extracts taken from my *Years Gone By* magazines of ten years, or so, ago. I hope that their inclusion here will enhance the enjoyment to be had from these old images of Canvey Island.

Introduction

Canvey Island is but a good stones throw from its neighbour, Benfleet, and today poses few problems for those of its residents bent on reaching the mainland. Not for us the hazard of using the slippery stepping stones while the tide is low, or planning our visits around the tide-tables.

What we take for granted was once an enormous problem for people, large vehicles and animals crossing the creek. Cars, carts and coal waggons were abandoned, caught out by incoming tides. Unguarded moments would sometimes result in cows and horses being swept away from their drivers. Ferrymen, whose presence was so very necessary, carved out a rough living charging passengers a penny to take them, often shivering in winter, back and forth at all hours.

Little wonder then that all of the island's people celebrated with street parties when the very first bridge was officially opened. The Colvin Bridge, named after the Lord Lieutenant of Essex, Brigadier-General R.B. Colvin, C.B. was declared open on 21 May 1931, exactly a year after the Brigadier officiated at the pile driving ceremony.

The swing bridge had been the dream of Revd Hayes, one of many he laboured to turn into reality for the community he loved. Sadly, he was never to see its completion.

Frederick Hester was another man with a vision. Some declared him an eccentric, but most thought him an entrepreneur. Call him what you will, but to his great credit he was the very first to develop the Island as a holiday resort. His imagination extended to building the most spectacular 'Greenhouse' covering an area of six square miles. He named it Winter Gardens and filled the glass conservatories with exotic fruits and plants. Peacocks ran free there and fish swam lazily around in ponds and under fountains. A Dutch bazaar, shopping alcoves, refreshment room and statuettes all added to its attraction. Today, only the name survives, as an adopted title for a modern housing estate.

Hester's walk around Canvey must surely have tired him, for he was also responsible for the laying of a metal mono-rail. Driven by horse-power, it took day-trippers part-way over the island and through his special Winter Gardens. Many of his schemes included something of the island's Dutch heritage and even now we have a legacy of Dutch names given by Frederick Hester to a number of Canvey's older roads.

The Dutch, of course, formed one of the island's earliest communities. Unlike their predecessors, they engineered to drain the island and under the guidance of Cornelius Vermuyden, keep the sea from invading the land. As payment for their great work some of the Dutch accepted land instead of cash payments and began to settle here. Julius Sludder, who by

1622 owned a considerable amount of land, may well have been responsible for the building of our curious Dutch Cottage in 1618.

Just a short walk away, we find ourselves at 'The Village'. It was here that in 1889 we would have cheered as part of a crowd gathered to witness the very first bucket drawn from the Village pump. It became the favourite meeting place for many islanders, a focal point where they could exchange tales and gather their water. Thanks to the good Revd Henry Hayes, the thatch cottage pump bore the inscription 'Whosoever drinketh of the water that I shall give him shall never thirst'. This very important landmark and the Village school, built earlier in 1874, both owed their existence to the efforts of the Reverend. The timber-framed place of education, that years later became the Village hall, stood opposite St Katherine's Church.

Like the first school, the first church was also made of wood. No less than four churches have stood on the site where the present building stands and during the early years its presence was to become a bone of contention between the Dutch and the English. Its use today serves as a memorial to the past, for it is Canvey's Heritage Centre.

As we leave the churchyard and the village behind, we are reminded that modern Canvey has indeed arrived. At the junction of Long Road and Furtherwick Park Road a very different view of the Haystack public house greets our eyes from when Madam French was its first landlady. In all its modern day glory the summer months now see it through a profusion of colour. Floral baskets suspended outside the doors and windows are dazzling in their brilliance. How very different from the days before those roads were made up and when the Haystack were nothing more than a single storey converted bus garage partnered by Madam French and her companion Mr Dillaway.

Our journey as we travel around the island's network of roads would take us close to the lake. Like an eye in the face of Canvey, a pool of colour hides a timeless history that dates back to Roman times. Only fish and eels are sought there today, though once this was a thriving oyster bed providing a staple diet for the poorer inhabitants of the island.

Next to the Village, Leigh Beck at Canvey's point was the next most highly populated area on the island. The road leading to it was part of the original sea wall and houses sprang up by its sides. These were unusual in as much as they were raised on stilts, to meet up with the height of the old High Street. The area changed its appearance, and many would say for the better, when in 1927 the road was lowered and the duck-board bridges providing access to the houses were well and truly made redundant.

The 'Point', the place where the High Street runs out, was for many years a source of interest to the Romans and, it is said, the Celts before them. Evidence is still uncovered today of Roman occupation. Fragments of pre-Roman and Roman pottery are still being unearthed during building works.

It was thought the Romans formed some kind of beacon at the point to warn against the perilous mud flats that have always existed there. In the nineteenth century a mechanical structure was erected, The Chapman Lighthouse. It was demolished in 1957 after the sea had taken its toll and put it in danger of collapse. If we look out to sea there today, 800 yards offshore, a single bell-buoy marks the spot.

Turning to the right and walking the modern sea wall, we come to the island's Esplanade. It is here at the sea front that visitors in the '50s enjoyed Andrew's Grand Amusement Arcade, a boating-pool, donkey rides and winkles for tea. In winter is was like any other seaside town, a little bleak, with the sea lashing mercilessly at our shores. Like any other ... until the terrible floods of 1953. A combination of freak winds and unusually high tides breached the sea walls, causing fifty-eight deaths and enormous devastation to a unique community. This same community refused to be put asunder and desperately fought its way back to become what the island still is today, a place very close to its inhabitants hearts.

One
Years Gone By

The tides out, looking towards Canvey where a farmer herds his cows across the causeway, in 1918. A stackie, laden with hay, waits for the tide to come in.

A novelty postcard of 1908 picturing the Canvey Ferry.

Mr Theobald's punt loads up for the short trip to Canvey in 1921. Notice the advertising board for the Canvey Supply Company.

A new carriage for the Mono-Rail (which was soon to be electrified) arrived in Canvey in 1905. Unfortunately, the railway never came about as Frederick Hester became bankrupt in 1905 and his dream for Canvey was no more.

Midstream on the way to Canvey, at high tide, in 1924.

View of Canvey Creek in Many 1930. Folks can be seen crossing to the right to Benfleet. The picture was taken at the time of the pile driving ceremony for the new Canvey Bridge, which opened to traffic in May 1931.

The Calvin Bridge was the first one to be built. It was second hand, cost £15,000 and was erected in 1930

The masses swarm across the new Canvey Bridge in 1931. Before this time the ferry boats sailed across at high tide, and when the tide was out, Islanders used the stepping stones to cross. After 1931 the ferry boats were no more.

The first car across the new Canvey Bridge in 1931.

Canvey's new bridge, just prior to its completion in 1930. Notice the last phase to go in at the centre, and the causeway to the right, with ferry boats still in operation.

THE BRIDGE, CANVEY ISLAND.   H.675.

Everything comes to a halt as barges pass through Canvey Bridge in 1934.

A view from the mainland overlooking the newly completed bridge, 1931. This postcard shows Waterside Farm in the background

Who will remember the Old Ferry Tea Rooms at the Bus Terminal on the Benfleet side of the bridge? When it fell into disuse it became the site for a car park at 2s a day. Today it is landscaped verges.

Waterside Farm in 1926 with outbuildings and pond, was the home of farmer Leach. Parts of this building are still being used as a council depot.

Picking up passengers for Canvey on Sea, at Waterside Farm bus stop. The cottages opposite are still there today.

Two

The Village

A rare picture of Ye Olde Dutch Cottage, 1618, taken in May 1920. The image is unusual because it puts the date of the building as 1604 and not 1618 as usually believed. In the past the Dutch Cottage was used as tea rooms.

The Dutch Cottage in 1928.

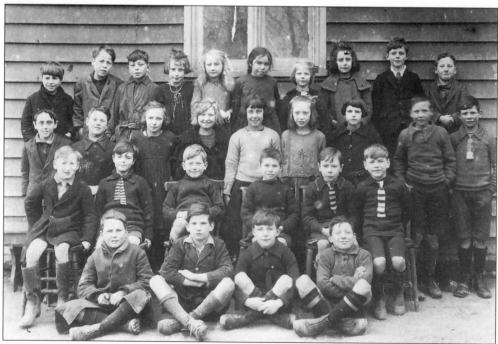

Village school class of 1924. The timber-framed school was opened in 1874 by Revd Hayes and closed when Long Road School (now William Read) was opened as a secondary school. Most of these pupils were transferred to Long Road.

This stone commemorates the first school and parish hall of Canvey Island, which stood on the site of Village Hall Close.

The village school, 1910. 'In 1874, Canvey's very first school was assembled opposite St Katherine's Church. A timber-framed building, its existence was solely due to the result of improvements for the community under the guidance of the Revd Hayes. It was closed when Long Road School, now William Read Infant and Junior School, was opened as a secondary school. This well known landmark was then put to use as a village hall and social events and church meetings regularly took place there until the fire, which almost completely gutted the building. The cause of the fire, a mystery at the time, appeared to have started in the chair store, burning clear through the floorboards. Strong winds helped to fan the flames and the blaze was reported to be seen at the top of Essex Way. Praise was given to the Canvey Firemen at their swift turnout by the mainland fire officers and undoubtedly their speed saved the hall's complete destruction, though substantial damage resulted in a £2,000 appeal being launched. The hall was only partially insured and this amount was estimated as needed against excess repairs. Sadly another piece of Canvey's history is no longer there'.

The Village School. This photograph taken at the turn of the century shows a number of pupils standing outside the wooden school. The teacher, dressed in severe black stands with hands clasped underneath the bell which is shortly to be rung for the afternoon session.

Inside view of St Katherine's Church, 1910.

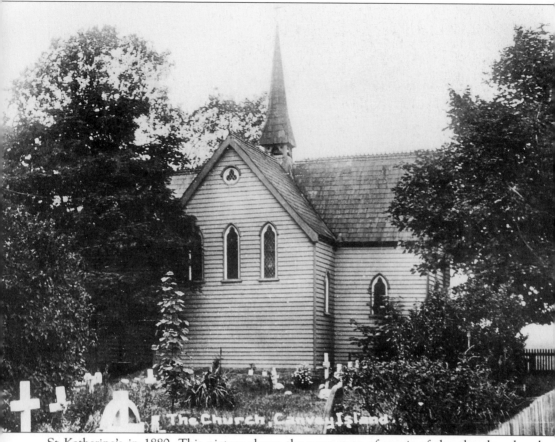

The Church, Canvey Island

St Katherine's in 1880. This picture shows the poor state of repair of the churchyard and boundary fence. The churchyard has now been extended on both sides and to the rear.

'Between the early 1600s and the late 1800s no less than four churches have stood on the site where St Katherine's stands today. The Dutch originally bought religion to the Island when they petitioned the King to be allowed to worship in their own tongue. Permission was given and the Dutch workers were responsible for the very first structure built in 1631. This was a chapel made of wood. At this time, the English community had to travel the long distance to Benfleet for their prayers, and approached the Dutch to be allowed to share their place of worship. The Dutch refused and this led to much disagreement between the two denominations resulting in skirmishes. However, the Dutch were successful in retaining the keys to the church. The Chapel was finally demolished in 1712 when many of the Dutch had returned to their homeland and it had fallen into disrepair. No resident Minister was available at this time and so it became reasonable to close the church up for the winter months when travel was more difficult. Payment of £10 was made, however, to the appointed visiting minister for twenty sermons per annum to be carried out in summer months. There is evidence to suggest that considerably less actually took place. Because of the erratic services, a flag was flown from the church steeple to indicate when worship would take place. This was thought to have twofold interest as it was also a warning of occupation to local smugglers who used the sanctuary, unofficially of course, to store their contraband in the Minister's absence. The new church, rebuilt in 1845, was for some reason named St Peter's. Canvey's population had grown considerably and, in 1872, the island was appointed a curate in charge - namely the Reverend Henry Hayes. He was later termed vicar when Canvey was declared an ecclesiastical parish.'

Those who lift a pint regularly in Canvey's King Canute may be interested to know that formerly it was known as The Red Cow, and once looked as it did in the picture above, along with the old village pump.

The newly built Red Cow public house in the shape you see it today. It was re-named The King Canute after the 1953 floods.

The village pump under construction in 1889. Before the pump was constructed the residents of the Island had to rely on water butts for all their water supplies.

THIS WELL PROVIDED FOR THE USE OF THE
INHABITANTS OF CANVEY ISLAND BY PUBLIC
SUBSCRIPTION AIDED BY A CONTRIBUTION
FROM THE CORPORATION OF THE CITY OF LONDON
WAS OPENED BY THE CHAIRMAN OF THE
PORT SANITARY COMMITTEE ON DEC 5TH 1889
AND IS VESTED IN THE UNDERSIGNED
AS A PERMANENT COMMITTEE

HENRY HAYES *vicar* }
WILLIAM COLLINGRIDGE *MD* } EX OFFICIO
ABRAHAM MANNING
ARTHUR MAYHEW CLARK

The village pump was opened on 5 December 1889, by the chairman of the Port Sanitary Committee, as this plaque shows.

Another look at the pump in 1910 and in the background, George Woods, confectioner. The shop today is an insurance office.

THE VILLAGE AND POST OFFICE, CANVEY ISLAND.

The village post office in 1908, run by J. Woods. The view looks down Haven Road and all the buildings, except the village pump, still stand today.

A water butt is filled at the village pump in 1913. The building in the background is now the District News Office.

The entrance to the village, 1913.

Brown's Bakers/Café, situated on the corner of Haven Road, was, along with Steven's Bakery, the first on the Island. Pictured are daughters, Beryl (left), Pat (centre) and June (right). Mr Brown ran three farms on Canvey and Beryl was born at Brickhouse Farm. All the daughters still live on Canvey today. The building today houses an insurance office.

The Dutch Cottage in Haven Road, used here as a private dwelling in 1948.

The second of the Dutch Cottages dated 1621. This stands in Haven Road and for much of its life has been a private dwelling.

Another view of the Dutch Cottage in Haven Road.

The Vicarage in Haven Road. In recent years it is more commonplace to find petrol tankers along this stretch of road. The building has been demolished to make way for council bungalows.

Ye Olde Village Pump in 1912, with The Red Cow public house, the Blacksmith and Farm in the background. The village shop is on the right. This building still stands today, but the village pump was pulled down in September 1937 to meet requirements of the Ministry of Transport.

The Lobster Smack, 1905, with a horse and trap outside. Standing in the doorway are sailors from the coastguard station.

30

How about a pint? The Lobster Smack in 1920.

THE LANDING STAGE, HOLE HAVEN. 1903.

The landing stage at Hole Haven where the fishermen loaded their catch in the 1930s.

The Coastguard Cottages in the 1920s in Hole Haven which was situated opposite the Lobster Smack public house. Today the cottages have been refurbished and are private dwelling houses.

The Coastguard Station with the cottages, 1923.

The Kynock Hotel, opened in 1900, never had a clock in the Clock Tower. For some years George Pickett was the manager. The building was constructed for £3,000, after many delays in building, a cost which was £1,000 over budget. The hotel was demolished in 1960 after being used for offices by London and Coastal.

French tanker *President Sergent* at Canvey oil jetty.

Powells' Store in 1925 stood at the end of Central Avenue. The shop catered for the residents of Winter Gardens and it was typical of the many stores at that time that sold just about everything. The Powell company also had other premises - a popular restaurant at the rear of Benfleet Station and a refreshment hut on the Canvey side of the bridge.

The Winter Gardens Club. Just one of the many clubs on Canvey in the 1920s and 1930s, situated in Central Avenue next to Powell Stores.

Three

Kingdom By The Sea

The King of Canvey in 1902, with his subjects, at what must have been Canvey's first carnival. This picture was taken next to Frederick Hester's Swedish bungalow in the Winter Gardens.

'It was without doubt a time to escape into the ridiculous, your only passport necessary, an extreme sense of humour. I am referring to those days in the very early 1900s when Islanders, albeit the minority, declared Canvey a separate Kingdom and announced it an individual monarchy. Their constitution demanded a 'King', house of notables and house of commoners. A very popular man at the time and one duly elected for the role of monarch, was Colonel Edward Clarke. He was (late of the King's Royal Rifles), a resident and owner of the 'haunted house' and a man whose personality and sense of the comical was recognised as being totally inexhaustible. His majesty ruled with a firm hand and declared that in the absence of a theatre, parliament, over which he most graciously presided would supply the ground for local humour and instigate ludicrous situations to spring forth. All this was doubtless taken in the spirit with which it was intended and debates over Imperial, Local and Social topics were encouraged to created a vast amount of merriment. Costume befitting the occasion was designed, not unlike the Arabian-style trouser, only sporting a heavy print. Tops resembled a blouse, with sleeves long and flouncy, bearing a collar similar to that of a sailor's at the rear, although cape-like over the front of the shoulder. A hat with plume completed the outfit. This mode of dress was worn only by the 'King' and members of his Notables while 'faithful Commoners' would have to earn recognition by some nonsense or ability, at which times they would be rewarded with buttons, peacock feathers and multi-coloured waistcoats. When, having been overloaded with such commendations, 'in the due process of time', ultimate reward would be theirs when invited to join the fraternity of Notables and exalted by the 'King', were sent to 'another place'. Funds paid into this mockery exchequer went to charitable purposes throughout the mimic Kingdom. How long the Island continued to have its humoristic reign is not clear to us, but one might guess that it phased out with the establishing of the Carnival'.

The 'King and his subjects' in 1902 outside Amsterdam in the Winter Gardens.

The Tower standing 50 ft high at the entrance of the Winter Gardens. Hester's tower supported the show bungalow where he would interview potential purchasers of his land. After his bankruptcy in 1905 the show bungalow was sold to a gentleman from London for his garden. The tower became unsafe and on inspection it became apparent that local residents had removed sections of it for firewood. It was demolished in 1909.

Two ladies rest after walking through the Botanical Gardens of the Winter Gardens, 1902.

The Botanical Gardens under glass, 1902, were a sight to behold. They stood next to Hester's Tower.

The Tea Rooms at the Winter Gardens, 1903.

Hester's Mono-Rail was able to carry twenty-four passengers across the Island in one of four horse-drawn carriages. The journey started at the Winter Gardens and ended at Shell Beach.

The Mono-Rail attendant dressed in Dutch costume to promote the sale of building plots, 1902. Postcards read 'Welcome to the Old Dutch Island of Canvey'.

THE MONO RAILWAY, CANVEY ISLAND. 1609.

The Mono-Rail mid journey, 1902.

The Swedish Bungalow, once the home of the Hester family.

A feel of the country once again, as we look down Winter Gardens path.

The Buffalo's meet at the village hall, 1924. The school was situated opposite St Katherine's Church.

The Fire Brigade party - can you spot some of these people around Canvey today? Pictured are: Roger Blackwell, Stanley Edwards, Steven Blackwell, Brian Whitcomb, Gordon Sanders, Philip Sanders, Geoff Barsby, Corrine Gill (nee Barsby), Shirley Grigsby (nee Barsby), Ricky Saunders, Heather Sanders, Janet Barsby and Ron Griffiths.

British Legion Concert Party during the war in 1939. Taken at the Old Premier Club Lakeside corner, they are front row, left to right: Jean Wallcar, Elsie O'Dare, Kit C. Lee, ? Claydon. Back row: Alice Jarvis, Lou Ward, Ethel Vincent, Flo Whelan, Emmy Clee, -?-.

BATHING POOL, CANVEY ISLAND.

The bathing pool at Thorney Bay, with the first café run by Mr Grout and boats that were hired out from the beach. Today the boats and café are gone - who said things change for the better?

The open air stage where Georgette's Juveniles put on stage shows, once a week throughout the summer. The stage is no longer there.

The Red Cross on Parade at Thorney Bay tent camp before the caravan site sprang up to accommodate the holiday maker. Families would fetch their tents to Colonel Fielders open air camp and hire a pitch.

Canvey Carnival with a Dutch theme in the early 1950s. Pictured here are Mr Chambers (back), Mrs Leach, Mrs Nightingale, Don Quinn (postman).

Pictured is another example of Canvey's beauty. Carnival queen Maureen Burder (as she was) was a little evasive about her exact age and would only give us an approximate date of around 1959, for the photograph. Don't worry Maureen, we really do believe you!

Another of Canvey's past carnival queens who still lives on the Island today, Joan Platten (as she was), 1956.

Carnival baby show in 1956. With queen Pamela Thipthorpe. On the left of the picture is nurse Morgan and Dr Craig. Also pictured are Dr and Mrs Lintner.

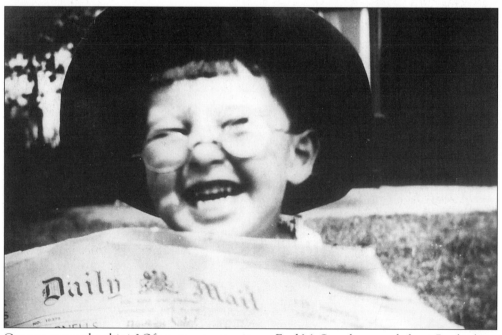

Can you guess who this is? Of course you can, it was Fred McCave here aged about 7, who later owned the *Canvey News*.

The Emelia Blackwell playgroup in 1978. The children today would be around 23 years old - are you among them?

Dick Knight, one of Canvey's first ambulance drivers, seen pictured with his Ford ambulance, the third of Canveys ambulances. The first ambulance was a Crossley Chevrolet. Do you recognise the building? It is the new Canvey Out Patients Clinic. The ambulance station was on the far right and the fire station on the far left. The council offices were in the centre and above.

Canvey Fire Station showing, from the left, retained firemen Ken Macquerie, Sony Blackwell, Bill Hall, Geoff Barsby and George Blackwell lining up for duty.

The Fielder's Bungalows on the Southwick Estate.

£250

All **BUNGALOWS** wired for Electric Light, Heating & Wireless. Gas Laid on.

FIELDER'S BUNGALOWS

PRICES include:
FREEHOLD LAND ROADS SANITATION
MAIN WATER GAS & ELECTRIC LIGHT

EASY TERMS ARRANGED

Visitors to Canvey **SOUTHWICK ESTATE**
should inspect the
where these Bungalows are now obtainable

Send Post Card for Illustrated Brochure to

**FIELDER ESTATES
(Canvey) LIMITED,**
HIGH ST., LAKESIDE CORNER,
CANVEY
'Phones: CANVEY 6
"   45
"   55
Telegrams: " Fielder, Canvey."
We are open all day on Satur-
days and Sundays

£295

Do you fancy a bungalow for £250 with sanitation, mains water, gas and electric light? Some of the houses on the Southwick Estate have been modernised, but many look the same today as they did then.

William Reed School, built in 1927 after the village school closed. First named Canvey Junior and Secondary School, later it was called William Reed (after its first headmaster). The school has since been modernised and now bears no resemblance to the one in this picture.

William Reed School, class of 1932. Ken Macquerie is in the back row, to the right, wearing a hat.

Denim Road in 1926, before its construction.

Harvest time on Canvey meant a great deal of manual work as there was little modern machinery.

Fred Knight with his hay wagon.

52

Old Canvey ambulance with crew, in 1951.

The Catholic Church in Long Road in the 1950s.

The bungalow, Linstoke. One of the many bungalows on Canvey.

The Convent of the Good Shepherd. The sisters of the convent would advertise regularly for orders of work, these could be frocks, coats, hats or fancy bags. Prices were given upon application for home baked toffee, coconut ice and other confectionery.

Four

Furtherwick Road

The ATC at Canvey Drill Hall, thirty-eight years ago. Revd Fleetwood far left, Peter Owens (officer in charge of 21875Q), John Clavio (centre), Peter Ware (with cap), other faces still about today, in the picture are: Alan Boyce, Michael English, Bill Newgent, Bryant Goodkind, Peter Glen, Ron Griffiths, Tony Kemp.

Mr Matthews stands in the doorway of Matthews & Chiles Estate Agents, in the 1930s. It stood next to the Radio Electric Company at the Haystack Corner.

Furtherwick Road, looking towards Lakeside, before the school was built in 1949/50. The shop on the right is now a chinese takeaway. On the parade on the left stood Vandersteens fish shop, which is now Islander's fish bar.

Inside the Rio Cinema, during the war years. It has now been converted into a bingo hall.

Nurse Morgan in 1950. Over thirty years she brought many of the Island's residents into the world. The photograph on the dresser is of Mrs Edith Fisk, who brought Nurse Morgan to Canvey in 1947.

Five
Leigh Beck

Furtherwick Road looking towards the Haystack. On the right stands Fisk Builders, before Fisk Corner was built in the 1930s.

Furtherwick Farm looking towards the seafront. It stood approximately where the Job Centre stands today.

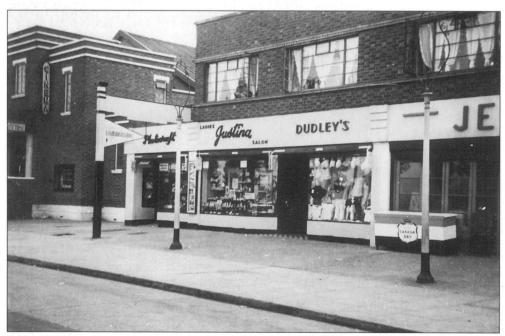

Justina Dudley's Jersey restaurant photographed in 1951. The Rio Cinema is on the left.

Madam French and Mr Dellaway, were the first landlords of the Haystack public house in the early 1920s.

The Haystack free house, converted from a single decker bus garage in the early 1920s.

Cubs and scouts and a mile of pennies on Whit Monday, opposite the Haystack public house in 1955. The event was organised for charity. Pictured here are several well known Canvey names including Mr Leach (farmer), Mr Girling and Terry O'Dare.

Fisk's Corner, in 1950. Notice that the top of the building today is different. The top tier was dismantled in 1958.

Mr Fred Fisk, builder, 1958. Fred's father, William Fisk, came to Canvey as the principal lighthouse keeper for Trinity House where he worked from 1913 to 1918. Fred's son, John, started John Fisk Estate Agents.

A fancy dress parade gathering at the Haystack in the early 1920s opposite Fisk Builders (now Fisks Canvey). Notice the unmade Furtherwick Road.

Canvey Rangers and Guides photographed in 1949 when off to a Chelmsford rally.

Photocraft Studios situated next to the Rio Cinema in Furtherwick Road. Through the war years it was opened as a canteen for the Forces by the W.V.S. The photograph dates from 1948.

Dale House, Furtherwick Road. It was the residence of the Fisk family in 1935, was later sold to Dr Mackachec and is now a day nursery.

Arthur and Elsie Lesadd at a topsy turvy night at the Haystack in 1936.

Topsy turvy dance night at the Haystack again, believed to be in the 1930s. It is hard to believe, that this is the Revd Stanley in drag!

Central Wall Road, Canvey, featuring Cherry stores in earlier times.

The properties along Canvey Lake, looking towards Benfleet, in 1919.

The building known as The Lighthouse in the 1920s situated in front of Oysterfleet public house. It was built by Captain Gregson as a home for his mother-in-law in order to keep her, it is said, out of the house! Sadly, the house did not have a preservation order on it and was demolished to make way for the new development of the Oysterfleet.

Tea Room at the Girls Bungalow in 1918. The bungalow stood on Lakeside Path near the Oysterfleet public house.

The cubicals next to the Girls Bungalow in the 1920s provided extra accommodation for the girls.

The playing grounds at the Girls Bungalow in 1910. The bungalow was run by Miss Clara James, for the benefit of 'overworked and overstrained' girls.

Harry Gayland and Mable Bicknell (née Webb) outside Canvey Service Station in the High Street. Somerfield supermarket now stands on this site.

Hazel Fisheries in the High Street was run by the Hopton family. Somerfield now stands on the site.

Canvey Football Club, 1952. Pictured with the players is Reg Holland, far left, and Derek James, far right.

It was certainly a grand occasion when Sidney Altermans shopping arcade was officially opened in 1955. Locals turned out in large numbers, curious and eager to purchase bargains. Altermans Shopping Arcade stood where the Knightswick Centre is today.

This house was in Somnes Avenue in 1956 and had it's own pond, a haven for injured swans and ducks.

The Nut Shell Café sold 'roast beef and veg', for 10p. This photograph shows Mr Pitt with two other members of his family, who also sold Canvey rock. The Nut Shell stood where Del Card Shop stands today.

The Rendezvous Club, run by proprietors Mr and Mrs Went, was situated in Larup Avenue. It later burned down.

Boheima Hall gave Canvey its first picture house.

'Once the main hall on Canvey island, Bohemia Hall was erected in approximately 1902. In its day it served the community well, acting as theatre, assembly room, conventicle, village hall, club room, cinema, headquarters for the Home-Guard and finally a factory, its list is endless. Before its demolition, Bohemia Hall could be found just before the approach to Small Gains Corner. Today, the site is a housing estate. It may well be remembered for its Bazaars, Armistice Services and stage performances, in particular Zoe Hammet's talented youngsters dancing their way through the Christmas pantomime, but possibly more so for its early vaudeville shows with performers Lux and Gay (theme song - 'How Are Yer?') and the very popular appearances of silent movies. Long before the Rio, Bohemia Hall was Canvey's first cinema. The quality of viewing was far from crystal clear. Often stars such as Charley Chaplin, Mary Pickford, Harold Lloyd and Tom Mix seemed to be acting throughout constant rain and snow storms due to the severe scratch marks on film. None-the-less they were happy days when people were glad to see anything without a single complaint. These were not the days of the plush curved back seat and sloping floor, quite the contrary, seats were hard and one would have to bob between shoulders to see anything at all. However, it did have its own air conditioning, an aircraft propeller from the 1914-18 war suspended from the ceiling. This novel idea was introduced by Mr Henry Pettit who had served in the war. Henry was responsible for the running of the cinema and the hiring of films. With the early silent movies came the captions underneath, and not always did the appropriate words run in time with the picture. The seventeenth century sea-faring *Captain Blood* was one such film. In a scene where the fearsome swashbuckling Captain was giving chase to another sailing ship the text read the command 'Full steam ahead'. However, the hilarity that arose because of it meant that it was still a good investment and Mr Pettit would repeat the performance again the next week. Local businesses had their advertisement printed boldly on the safety curtain to be read before and after the film showing, and during the interval when the house lights went up for refreshments and lemonade (made from powder) could be bought. Where children were concerned, it seems little changes over the years, some of the more daring sneaked in for nothing through a hole in the back wall to watch *Rin Tin Tin* or some similar feature. Henry Pettit was once heard to call upon the audience for volunteers to help chuck the little rascals out. Today we take our ABC's and Odean's for granted with their luxury seating and high quality block busters but I guarantee just as much enjoyment was had from seeing Mary Pickford (once even in her bloomers), in Bohemia Hall then, as could be gained from watching Arnold Schwartzenegger today'.

74

Redman & Sons Estate Office in the High Street, 1950.

Soldiers on leave in the war years at the Corner Club. On the piano is Herbert Bailey, grandfather of the author.

The last boat in Small Gains Creek before it was damned and drained in 1939.

Small Gains Creek. Its hard to believe that today football is played where house boats and sailing boats were once commonplace.

Small Gains Corner. Small Gains Farm stood on the corner with the house occupied by the chauffeur of H. Price Powell, a local councillor and man of property.

Gains Farm, looking towards Leigh Beck from Small Gains Corner, 1923. The farm was owned by Mr Price Powell.

The lowering of the High Street, looking toward Small Gains. The road was lowered in the early 1920s to bring the old sea wall to the level of the buildings. Before this time the buildings were set on stilts so that residents could use the old sea wall as a road. Also notice the railway line built to carry materials to and from the site.

The Express Laundry, situated in Small Gains. After moving from Knightswick, Bill Byron and his wife Alice, seen in the photograph, ran Canvey's first Launderette. The introduction of self-service style laundries made these businesses unviable.

The Kynock's Club, ladies darts team. All these ladies are now deceased. The club stood in the High Street opposite the War Memorial Hall.

Zoe Hammet in the 1930s. Zoe formed the Island's first dance school. Among her many pupils was Queenie Gray (née Harris) who today is the principal of Georgettes Juvenile's Dance and Stage School. Zoe died in 1941, aged only 34 years.

Uncle Sam's Minstrels, 1933. All blacked up, they were popular with the Islands visitors.

The Traveller's Rest (then Hall), stood for many years opposite Hope Road in the High Street.

The Settlement had been built from relics of the historic Chapman House. It was the home of William Wilberforce, abolitionist, in 1912.

St Annes Church could be reached by bridge from the High Street in 1924.

The Wilberforce Bungalow. When a later resident (who is thought to have owned the bungalow) passed away, his request that he should never leave the home, that in life he loved so much, was observed to the letter. When it was next decorated, the bungalow was pebbledashed, and his ashes were poured into the mixture.

The Bungalows in Leigh Beck, just before the road was lowered, 1924. Notice the bridges giving access to the house from the road, the old sea wall.

Pictured in 1961, this is Canvey Baptist Church, much as it still looks today.

This photograph, dating from 1920, shows the very first Canvey market, situated opposite Steven's Bakery, in Canvey High Street. It is amusing to see that 'admission was free', as an encouragement to enter the premises.

Whittier Hall Institute was built in 1926, providing recreational and educational facilities at Leigh Beck.

An advertisement for Canvey's Market in 1925. It was situated in the High Street where Gafzell Drive stands today.

The Canvey Hall, at Leigh Beck 1911. It appears that a womens' group have been marking an event with a ceremonial tree planting.

The Total Abstinence Union, Canvey Island Branch. Meetings were held in Whttier Hall in the 1930s.

Total Abstinence Society Concert at Whittier Hall, 1948.

The Reliance Bakery in 1934 was run by the Steven's family and stood next to Mitchell's Library. To the right is the Canvey Studio where you could have your films developed and printed.

An early photograph of the Admiral Jellicoe. The cars in the car park are different, but the Jellicoe remains almost unchanged.

Frederick Hester purchased Leigh Beck Farm for £2,000. At Leigh Beck he sunk an artesian well fashioned on the design of a water mill. It soon became the envy of all his neighbours who only had unreliable garden wells or had to trek three miles to the village pump. Some became customers of Leigh Beck Farm and willingly paid 2s 6d a quarter (12p) for their supply.

Chapman Lighthouse. In 1951 it celebrated its 100th anniversary with flags flying.

Bill Oddy, Commodore of the Island Yacht club in 1951 with the 100th anniversary plaque. It was presented to Chapman Lighthouse in honour of its century of service.

Six
Sea Front

Canvey's Shell Beach was the ideal getaway for day trippers from the Smoke, and they flooded in by the hundreds during the 1930s.

An early photograph of the Casino before the construction of the road and the Monico.

The cycle park on Canvey sea front, 1954. Notice Cafe Rose in the background which was run by the Thorne Family.

An ariel view of the sea front and beach, before the Meadway Estate was built. Marine Garage and Pals Parade are visible, top left.

The Welcome Hut and sea wall looking towards the bay and before the Labworth Cafe.

The Labworth Cafe and market stalls in the 1930s, before the Monico was built. Notice the old cars in the car park.

Canvey sea front in the 1960s. The model village is on the left but is no longer there today.

Another photograph of the new sea wall and beach in 1956. In the distance the Bay Country Club can be seen (later the Goldmine). Now demolished with flats standing in its place.

Solidified concrete blocks salvaged from the wreck of the SS *Benmore*, are scattered on the shore in 1908. Residents later salvaged them and used them in the foundations of their properties.

Concord which used to be a Easter Esplanade. The fenced off land here is now the road. The vacant ground (right) is now the sea front end of May Avenue. This property has been demolished and is a council open space.

The remains of Hester's Jetty in 1919. This area was a popular place for visitors.

This barren landscape attracted these visitors in 1912, but further up the coast they came for the beach.

An afternoon stroll in the 1940s with the Beach House and Sutherland's fair on the left and Tea Huts on the beach. None of the buildings shown in this picture are there today.

The Walter Cox Emporium in 1912 was a post office, cafe and grocers.

Canvey people loved fairgrounds and in 1926 holiday makers flocked to Sutherland's fair which stood at the end of the Sea View Road.

The Queensbury Bungalow built on Canvey Island. Note the viewing room/sun trap conservatory on the roof top.

The Bathing Huts at Shell Beach, were made of corrugated iron, 1924.

The Pavilion Tea Gardens on Canvey sea front in 1937.

A party of holiday makers shrimping at Shell Beach in 1922.

Day trippers to Canvey in the late 1940s. This car park is still in use today, next to Astairs.

The Labworth Cafe was never so busy as when the Royal Yacht Britannia passed by in the 1960s.

The pleasure yacht *Victoria* picking up a passenger in 1929.

Sailing down the river on a Sunday afternoon, well not quite! Canvey's boating pool was every bit as popular in its day as the casino.

The casino and boating pool, looking rather shabby here in the 1940s.

Sea View Road before its construction in the 1920s.

The same section of Sea View Road after its construction.

Pre-war joy rides were popular with the holidaymakers visiting Canvey. This two-seater plane ascended and returned to base next to Andrew's fair by the casino.

Hard work for the donkey in 1926, Reg and Burt Bishop are seen here with friends in Maurice Road.

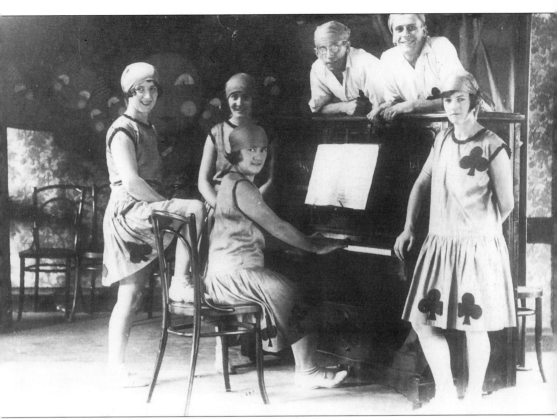

The Orange Pipps Concert Party at Smallgains Hall in 1930.

Sunset across the water, 1922.

Building a jetty for the Yatch Club in the 1940s. Sam Girling is the one wearing a hat.

One of the first bus companies on Canvey was owned by Mr Knight, seen here at Leigh Beck in around 1920.

W. McCave, took part in the English Open Table Tennis Championships at Wembley, in1950 when he was 24 years old.

Charles Hollingberry, all time Ten Pin Bowling record holder and player of Britain's first perfect game, at Basildon bowl, in 1962.

Residents of St Alphage, Harvest Road, Canvey in 1943.

The 14 Star Cafe and Tea Gardens, with an inset picture of the proprietors, in the 1930s.

Canvey Hall outing, 1911. Note the children's Sunday best bonnets.

After a day out at Canvey, people queue for a bus home, *c. 1950*. In the background is the Bay Country Club, which later became the Goldmine.

A Conservative Party dance in the mid 1950s. Among the faces are Sam Girling, the water rate collector and Mr and Mrs Manthorpe, all at the back, and in the front row, Bernard Braine, MP. Can you name anymore?

A north view of the Canvey Model Village, which was situated on the sea front, just below the Labworth Cafe.

Another view from Canvey Model Village.

Canvey Model Village's version of the Lobster Smack.

Canvey Model Village in 1948. The Model Village was situated next to the putting course.

The Chapman Lighthouse, viewed from the sea wall, with sailing boats carrying cargos up the Thames in 1910.

In the distance stands Chapman Lighthouse, 1930. This picture also shows the remnants of the old Dutch sea wall which had fallen into disrepair by 1830. Today's wall was built some 60 yards inland from here.

A tasty tea could always be purchased at Bond Stores, Leigh Beck, Canvey Island.

The beach and sea wall. Notice the sign for the Goldina Tea Rooms situated in the Station Road area. You had to cross a bridge to quench your thirst in the 1930s.

Mothers and toddlers at Whittier Hall in 1932.

The Canvey Brotherhood at Whittier Hall in the 1930s.

The elegant Ozonia Hotel, with its thatched roof, stood where Seaview Court stands today. Unfortunately the hotel was never commercially successful and many of its rooms were never occupied. On its ground floor was a small tea room.

Ozonia Hotel after the thatched roof had been replaced.

In 1928 Canvey seafront was full of places in which to eat and Marlborough House was considered one of the finest. It was a situated between Maurice Road and Keer Avenue and also provided rooms to rent.

Beach House and Sutherland's fair in 1933. Both have long since gone; only fishermen and those with boats use this area nowadays.

The *Summer Rose* loading holidaymakers for a trip around the lighthouse in 1948.

SEA WALL AND BEACH, CANVEY ISLAND.

Anyone for a jog! Looking towards the Point in 1942.

Seven

The Great Flood 1953

Houses being checked for survivors after evacuation in the 1953 flood.

Outside Canvey Clinic in 1953 looking towards Lakeside. The car on the right looks as if it has damp problems!. Notice the fire engines probably in use for pumping water out of houses.

The building of the sea wall after the 1953 flood. This photograph was taken in 1954 or 1955.

Outside Canvey Clinic in 1953 looking towards Lakeside. The car on the right looks as if it has been flooded. Notice the fire engines.

Relief workers fill sand bags at the Red Cow in 1953. The name was changed to the King Canute, after the water receded

Mr Liddiard used his kitchen chairs as stepping stones to get to the safety of higher ground.

The Green Glades Restaurant, situated where the Merco garage now stands. Mr and Mrs Liddiard were the proprietors.

The book concludes with a charming sequence of humorous postcards using illustrations of Canvey Island drawn by the artist known just as 'Phil.B' in the early 1930s.

WOULD YOU LIKE US TO "HEAVE TO" DAD?
NO MY LAD, I DON'T NEED ANY HELP ~~~

THIS FERRY IS PART OF THE THAMES I SUPPOSE?
I SHOULD SAY IT'S PART OF THE RED SEA